Pocket Watches

L'OROLOGIO DA TASCA

Leonardo L.
Gabriele k

CHRONICLE BOOKS

SAN FRANCISCO

First published in the United States of America in 1994 by Chronicle Books.
Copyright © 1988 by BE-MA Editrice.
All rights reserved. No part of this book may be reproduced in any form without
written permission from Chronicle Books.

Printed in Hong Kong.

Library of Congress Cataloging-in-Publication Data:

Leonardi, Leonardo.
    Pocket watches = l'Orologio da tasca / Leonardo Leonardi, Gabriele Ribolini.
    p.   cm. — (Bella cosa)
    Includes index.
ISBN 0-8118-0753-3
1. Pocket Watches — History.
I. Ribolini, Gabriele.   II. Title.   III. Title: Orologio da Tasca.   IV. Series.
TS542.L46 1994
681.1'14 — dc20   93-48527 CIP

Caption translation: Joe McClinton
Photography: Cesare Gualdoni
Cover photograph: Cesare Gualdoni
Cover and text design: Dana Shields, CKS Partners, Inc.
Production: Robin Whiteside

Distributed in Canada by Raincoast Books,
8680 Cambie Street, Vancouver, B.C. V6P 6M9

10   9   8   7   6   5   4   3   2

Chronicle Books
275 Fifth Street
San Francisco, California 94103

Introduction

*I*n the late fifteenth century there was the "drum": the first crude spring-powered watch with a single hand.

In time, the heavy cylindrical watch shapes softened into so-called onions and eggs. Cases became thinner and were adorned with refined engraving and colored enamels, while the movements inside were improved and made more accurate. Each timepiece became a minor masterpiece of mechanical engineering.

The pocket watch became the most prestigious of status symbols. At the height of its vogue, it was worn ostentatiously in the waistcoat pockets of the rich, suspended from imposing and elegant chains.

Our photographic panorama evocatively documents the basic stages in the evolution of these noble timepieces from 1700 to 1950.

The details illustrate the ingenious technique and patient care the watchmaker spent on his creations.

Silver Oignon with Shagreen Leather,

Toward the end of the seventeenth century, watches acquired a rounded shape, from which they became known as *oignons* (onions). From this period one typically finds a simple case hinged to the movement itself. The protective shagreen leather covering with silver studs forms an attractive decoration.

Oignon in argento con pelle di zigrino fine '600
Verso la fine del '600 gli orologi acquistarono una forma tondeggiante per cui furono chiamati Oignon (cipolloni). Tipica di questo periodo fu la cassa semplice che per mezzo di una cerniera costituiva un unico pezzo col meccanismo stesso. Il rivestimento di protezione in pelle di zigrino con i chiodi d'argento di fissaggio forma una piacevole decorazione.

Gold Oignon,

LATE 17ᵀᴴ CENTURY

*O*ne reason for the watch's ball-like shape was the indispensable fusee, a device that served to keep the spring force constant as the spring unwound.

Oignon in oro fine '600
L'orologio assume una forma di palla anche per la presenza indispensabile del conoide.
Questo dispositivo serviva a mantenere costante la forza della molla nelle varie posizioni di carica.

Silver Alarm Watch with Chimes and Date,

EARLY 18ᵀᴴ CENTURY

A rare example of a timepiece with a so-called complicated mechanism that indicates the day of the month, as well as the time. It also has an alarm, set by turning the inner dial counterclockwise. The fine protective case, covered in tortoise shell and typical of clocks intended for the Turkish market, has a finely perforated central band.

The count wheel, or locking plate, that controls the striking mechanism is clearly visible on the inside.

Orologio in argento a sveglia e suoneria a passaggio e calendario inizio '700
Raro esemplare di orologio con complicazione che segna il giorno del mese. Completato di sveglia a suoneria: la messa a punto della sveglia si ottiene girando il quadrantino interno in senso antiorario. La bella cassa di protezione rivestita in tartaruga, tipica degli orologi destinati al mercato turco, presenta una fascia centrale finemente traforata. All'interno ben visibile la ruota spartiora per il comando dei rintocchi della suoneria.

Skeleton Watch,

The craftsman's virtuosity found an excellent outlet in the skeleton watch. The artist applied all his skill and imagination in creating movements that were pared down to their barest essentials and embellished with tiny but precise decorations. The case was backed with glass, of course, so that everyone could admire his prodigious talent.

Orologio scheletrato primi del 700

Il virtuosismo dell'artigiano si manifestava negli orologi scheletrati. Qui la perizia dell'artista otteneva il massimo della sua fantasia nel creare dei meccanismi scarnificati nelle parti più essenziali ed ingentiliti da una minuziosa quanto precisa decorazione. Naturalmente il fondello era realizzato in vetro per dare la possibilità a chiunque di apprezzare tanto talento.

English Watch with Independent Dead Seconds,

Watches with so-called independent dead seconds were probably the forerunners of the chronograph. They first appeared in the early eighteenth century and characteristically had a large central hand which, when activated, moved one step around the dial every second. They had their own springs, barrels, and complete wheel trains independent from the main movement.

Orologio inglese a secondi morti indipendenti prima metà '700
Gli orologi cosiddetti a secondi morti indipendenti apparsi all'inizio del 700, furono probabilmente gli antesignani dei cronografi. Essi erano caratterizzati da una grossa lancetta centrale, che opportunamente innescata avanzava sul quadrante con uno scatto ogni secondo. Era fornita di una molla, un barilletto e un completo treno di ingranaggi del tutto indipendente dal meccanismo principale.

Silver Carriage Clock,

*I*n the eighteenth century, carriage clocks came into fashion. They were large and sturdy to withstand the harsh conditions of travel in those days. Typically, these were repeaters that struck the hour on command, usually when a chime mechanism was activated by pulling a small cord.

In the example here the silver outer case is embossed with a military scene. The attaching ring is quite strong and equipped with the shock-absorbing articulation commonly seen in carriage clocks.

Orologio in argento da carrozza epoca prima metà '700

Nel '700 divennero di moda gli orologi da carrozza, assai grandi e robusti, atti a sopportare le dure traversie di un viaggio di quell'epoca. Loro caratteristica era quella di essere a ripetizione, cioè dietro comando (di solito il tiro di una funicella metteva in movimento una suoneria) batteva le ore e i quarti. Nell'esemplare qui riprodotto la cassa esterna in argento è sbalzata e rappresenta una scena militare, mentre l'anello di aggancio è assai robusto e fornito della snodo tipico degli orologi da carrozza che doveva attenuare le scosse.

English Watch with Embossed Gold Outer Case,

This outer case of embossed gold is particularly fine. The outer case, rather than the watch case itself was embossed, since the embossing was so deep that the back of the outer case had to be lined with soldered sheets of metal foil. The artist's skill is evident not only in the decoration, but also in the use of four different shades of gold.

Orologio inglese con controcassa in oro sbalzato metà '700

Particolarmente pregevole questa controcassa in oro sbalzato. La tecnica dello sbalzato veniva applicata preferibilmente sulla controcassa anziché sulla cassa stessa. La profondità delle figure a sbalzo era tale per cui il fondo della controcassa doveva poi essere foderato con delle lamine saldate. Qui la perizia dell'artista risalta, oltre che dalla decorazione, anche dall'uso dell'oro in quattro colori diversi.

Enameled Pocket Watch with Chatelaine,

A stunning example of a watch with enameled decoration. The chatelaine, which came into style in the mid-eighteenth century, was an elaborate chain that allowed the watch to be hung from the belt, in full view. The watch case, the richness of decoration, the complexity of the chain, and the accessories attached to it (seals, winding keys, miniatures) were all indicators of the wearer's social status.

Orologio da tasca in smalto e chatelaine metà '700
Stupendo esemplare di orologio da persona con decorazione in smalto.
La chatelaine venuta di moda nella metà del '700 consisteva in una complicata catena che permetteva di appendere l'orologio alla cintura ben in vista.
Dalla cassa dell'orologio, dalla ricchezza delle decorazioni, dalla complessità della catena e dagli accessori (sigilli, chiavette di carica, miniature ecc.) che vi erano appesi si poteva risalire allo status sociale di chi li indossava.

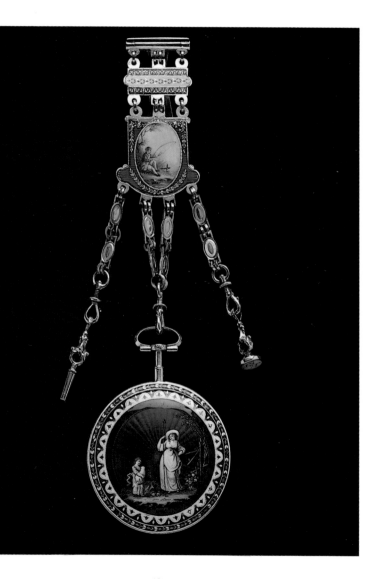

18-Carat Gold Watch with Enameled Case and Diamonds,

Beginning sometime after 1750, England, France, and Holland began to export a considerable number of highly prized movements to Switzerland. There, expert enamelers and jewelers had gathered after fleeing religious persecution in their own countries. Thus was born the famous Geneva school of jewelry.

Orologio in oro 18K con cassa smaltata e brillanti metà '700
A partire dalla seconda metà del '700 si iniziò un forte flusso di meccaniche di alto pregio costruite in Inghilterra, Francia e Olanda destinate alla Svizzera. Qui, infatti, scacciati dalle loro terre per motivi religiosi, si erano raggruppati abili smaltatori e gioiellieri che dettero vita alla famosa scuola di gioielleria ginevrina.

Chased Gold Clock with Miniature,

Late in the eighteenth century, enamel decoration tended to be confined to the center of the back of the case, where it was framed in a low relief of precious metal. The chatelaine in this example is particularly rich and finely worked, and includes two portraits of family members.

The watch was worn with the dial turned inward toward the waistcoat, so as to show off the decorated case, along with the chatelaine itself and all its rich enamel work.

Orologio in oro cesellato con miniatura seconda metà '700

Verso la fine del '700 la decorazione in smalto tende a restringersi ed occupare solo la parte centrale del coperchio posteriore, rimanendo così incorniciata da un bassorilievo di metallo prezioso. Estremamente ricca e di finissima lavorazione la chatelaine in questo esemplare che racchiude anche due ritratti di familiari. Indossato in questo modo, l'orologio aveva il quadrante rivolto verso il panciotto in modo che la parte in mostra era la cassa cesellata e decorata e la chatelaine in tutta la sua ricchezza di smalti.

English Carriage Clock with Alarm and Calendar,
MID TO LATE 18ᵀᴴ CENTURY

$\mathcal{A}$ carriage clock identifiable by the large articulated suspension ring and size of the cord activating the striking mechanism. The mechanism is "complicated" with a calendar showing the day of the month through a little window above the 6.

The balance cock and back plate are beautifully decorated, and the latter has exquisitely made support posts.

Orologio inglese da carrozza con sveglia e calendario epoca seconda metà '700
Orologio da carrozza che si identifica dalle dimensioni della cordicella di richiamo della suoneria e dall'anello di aggancio a snodo. Ulteriormente complicato dalla presenza del calendario che attraverso una finestrella posta sopra le 6 segna il giorno del mese. Finissima è la decorazione del coq e della platina posteriore i cui pilastrini di supporto sono di squisita fattura.

French Watch with Outer Case of Gold and Diamonds,

MID TO LATE 18ᵀᴴ CENTURY

Throughout the eighteenth century, the watch was enclosed in one or more outer cases. Since the winding hole on the watchcase proper allowed dust into the movement, a second case was a protective necessity. At first simple in design, these secondary cases very quickly became more decorative. This example is enameled with the portrait of a coquettish young lady, framed in diamonds.

Orologio francese con controcassa in oro e brillanti seconda metà '700
Durante tutto il '700 l'orologio si riveste di una o più controcasse di protezione. Difatti il foro di carica presente sulla cassa faceva penetrare la polvere nel meccanismo; di qui la necessità di una ulteriore scatola di protezione. In un primo tempo, semplici, queste controcasse ben presto cominciarono ad arricchirsi di decorazioni. In questo esemplare la cassa è ornata di uno smalto raffigurante la civettuola effige di una giovinetta e contornata di pietre preziose (diamanti).

French Repeater,
MID TO LATE 18ᵀᴴ CENTURY

A repeater can often be recognized by the length of the ring's neck. As might be guessed, the striking mechanism was activated by pressing the ring.

Orologio francese a ripetizione della seconda metà del '700
Spesso ci si può accorgere che un orologio è a ripetizione dalla lunghezza del collo dell'anello. Infatti si intuisce che l'anello premuto serve ad innescare il meccanismo della ripetizione.

Gold Watch with Enameling and Pearls,

MID TO LATE 18TH CENTURY

$\mathcal{T}$oward the last quarter of the eighteenth century, watches with beautifully executed enameling became widespread. The enamel decoration was often further adorned with a ring of pearls or, more rarely, precious stones.

The outer case, which had otherwise been in use since 1640, was typically used in this period to protect an exposed dial. Since the winding pin was on the dial, there was no way to cover it with a normal glass.

Orologio in oro con smalti e perle seconda metà '700
Verso l'ultimo quarto del '700 vi fu una larga diffusione di orologi in smalto di ottima fattura ove spesso la decorazione a smalto era ulteriormente impreziosita da una corona di perle o più raramente di pietre preziose.
Tipico di questo periodo è l'utilizzo della controcassa, per altro utilizzata a partire fin dal 1640, a protezione del quadrante interiore. Infatti la presenza del perno di carica sul quadrante, impediva di essere protetto da un normale vetro.

Quarter Repeater with Enamel,

LATE 18ᵀᴴ CENTURY

$\mathcal{T}$he obvious advantage of the watch over the sundial is that it could signal the time even at night. But one still had to be able to see it, or at least to hear it, in the dark.

Repeaters were invented for this purpose. One only had to press the stem and the watch would strike the hours and quarters. The classically inspired enamel is of very fine workmanship.

Orologio a ripetizione ore e quarti con smalto fine '700

Il grande vantaggio dell'orologio fu di poter segnare l'ora anche di notte cioè quando le meridiane non funzionavano. Bisognava però poterli vedere o, se al buio, almeno sentirli. A questo scopo nacquero gli orologi a ripetizione: era sufficiente premere sul collo del gambo, per far battere le ore e i quarti. Di pregevole fattura lo smalto di ispirazione classica.

English Watch,

Although there were innumerable types of escapements, the verge type was undoubtedly the most widely used up through the 1700s. New developments in escapements arrived only toward the end of the century.

Shown here is one of the first examples of the anchor escapement, a system whose characteristic accuracy earned it wide use in watches.

Orologio inglese fine '700

Benché i tipi di scappamento siano stati innumerevoli, il più usato fu certamente, fino a tutto il '700, quello a verga. Soltanto sul finire del 18° secolo si assiste alla nascita di nuovi scappamenti.

Quello qui rappresentato è una delle prime realizzazioni di scappamento ad àncora, sistema che per gli orologi da persona ebbe larga applicazione per la precisione tipica di questo sistema.

Quarter Repeater,

LATE 18TH CENTURY

*A*s construction techniques became more refined, the carriage clock was made smaller until it became a normal repeating pocket watch.

This example sounds the hours and quarters on command, with a hammer that strikes a bell inside the case. Not until the nineteenth century was the bell replaced by a gong, tuned steel bars that chimed when struck with a hammer. This innovation is attributed to the famous watchmaker Breguet.

Orologio a ripetizione ore e quarti fine '700

A mano a mano che le tecniche costruttive diventavano più raffinate, l'orologio da carrozza si fece più piccolo, e divenne un normale orologio da tasca.

L'esemplare nella fotografia suona a richiesta le ore e i quarti. I suoni sono ottenuti con colpi di martelletti su una campana fissata all'interno della cassa. Soltanto con l'inizio dell'800 la campana fu sostituita dal gong, cioè barre metalliche di acciaio armonico che percosse dal martelletto emettevano il suono della ripetizione. Questa innovazione è fatta risalire al famoso orologiaio Breguet.

Gold Watch with Fine Enamel,

LATE 18TH CENTURY

$\mathcal{B}$y the late eighteenth century, case decorations had become true works of art, as in this exquisitely refined example, whose enamel decoration is surrounded with an elegant twining motif.

Orologio in oro e smalto fine '700
La decorazione della cassa poteva arrivare, sul finire del '700, a creare delle vere e proprie opere d'arte, come questo esemplare di delicatissimo gusto la cui decorazione a smalto è contornata da un elegantissimo motivo a torciglione.

Gold Watch with Fine Enamel,

LATE 18TH CENTURY

*I*n the late eighteenth century, the entire back cover of a watch was enameled, making it a miniature painting. Here the scene depicts a pair of lovers in the neoclassical style dictated by contemporary fashion.

Orologio in oro con smalto fine '700
Alla fine del '700 lo smalto ricopre tutta la parte posteriore della cassa dell'orologio e diventa un vero e proprio quadro in miniatura. In questo caso, la scena rappresenta una coppia di innamorati che la moda dell'epoca impone di gusto neoclassico.

French Gold Watch with Sector Dial,

18TH CENTURY

This curious French watch has a dial decorated in sectors, with a return system indicating the hour. When the hour hand reached the first 6, it rapidly swept through a 180° arc, then continued normally back to the 12.

Orologio francese in oro con quadrante a settore del '700

Curioso orologio francese con quadrante a settore decorato a tre tornanti. Giunta sulle prime ore 6 la lancetta delle ore si sposta rapidamente di 180° per risalire verso le 12.

English Watch with Outer Case,

The richly decorated movement of this watch compensates for the simple outer case of smooth gold desired by the English market.

After opening the outer case, the watchcase proper and yet another protective dome, one finds a superb, delicately pierced balance cock, at the center of which is a diamond supporting the balance pivot.

Orologio inglese fine '700 con controcassa
Questo orologio compensa con un meccanismo ricco e decorato, la semplicità della cassa esterna in oro liscio come imponeva il gusto del mercato inglese. All'interno sotto la controcassa, la cassa ed una ulteriore calotta di protezione, appare una splendida coq finemente traforata al cui centro è posto un diamante a supporto dell'asse del bilanciere.

French Repeater with Automatons,

LATE 18TH TO EARLY 19TH CENTURY

Automatons were connected to little mechanisms which animated them when the watch chimed. They often took the form of little human figures or cherubs striking bells. The sound is actually emitted by the internal chime, with which the motions of the figure are synchronized.

Orologio francese a ripetizione con automi fine '700 inizio '800

Gli automi sono meccanismi collegati a delle figure che si animano con l'azionamento della ripetizione. Spesso vengono rappresentate delle forme umane o dei putti che battono su campane. Nella realtà il suono veniva emesso dalla campana interna, mentre la figura dell'automa era in sincronia col suono della ripetizione.

Gold Swiss Watch with Two Dials,

The turn of the nineteenth century saw the disappearance of sumptuous decoration as the Age of Enlightenment revived an appreciation for the technical features of the watch. The example here is the result of a major mechanical refinement that slimmed down the timepiece considerably. It has two dials for two separate time zones, plus a large hand for the independent dead seconds.

Orologio svizzero in oro a doppia ora inizio '800
Con l'inizio dell'800 scompaiono le decorazioni e l'illuminismo porta ad apprezzare il tecnicismo dell'orologio. L'esemplare qui fotografato è il risultato di un grosso affinamento meccanico tendente ad assottigliare il pezzo. Presenta un duplice quadrante per i due fusi orari separati e la grande sfera dei secondi morti indipendenti.

English Watch,

EARLY 19ᵀᴴ CENTURY

When the watchcase is hinged to the movement and the bezel, forming a single body divided into four components, the watch is called a folding piece. This feature, and even more so the gilt dial with raised gold numerals, was common in Victorian English watches.

Orologio inglese inizio '800

Quando la cassa è incernierata al meccanismo e alla lunetta portavetro, formando un unico corpo suddiviso in 4 componenti, l'orologio viene definito a ribaltina. Questa peculiarità, e più ancora il quadrante dorato con ore riportate dello stesso metallo prezioso, caratterizzano spesso gli orologi inglesi di epoca vittoriana.

Gold Vacheron Watch,

EARLY 19TH CENTURY

The Vacheron family was already building watches and watchmaking machinery in the late eighteenth century. An association with Mr. Constantin did not lead to the founding of Vacheron & Constantin until 1817, so this example dates from before that year. It offers an elegant silver dial with a center design and radial divisions.

Orologio Vacheron in oro inizi dell'800
La famiglia Vacheron costruiva già sul finire del '700 orologi e macchinari per la costruzione di orologi. Solo nel 1817, a seguito dell'associazione con il signor Constantin, nacque la Vacheron & Constantin. L'esemplare è quindi anteriore a questa data e offre un bel quadrante in lamina d'argento impreziosito da una decorazione centrale e da una suddivisione in spicchi a raggiera.

English Silver Watch,

TH CENTURY

Very simply designed watches with a smooth case and a rather squat ring-neck were typical of the English industry. Design criteria emphasized a sturdy movement and legible dial over any other aesthetic consideration.

Orologio inglese in argento inizio '800
Tipici della produzione inglese sono gli orologi molto semplici con cassa liscia e collo dell'anello piuttosto tozzo. I criteri di costruzione privilegiarono infatti la robustezza della meccanica e la leggibilità del quadrante su ogni altra concessione estetica.

Vacheron & Constantin Repeater,

BEFORE 1850

*O*ne of the first Vacheron & Constantin watches, traceable to the first half of the nineteenth century. By now the chime no longer uses a bell but gongs instead. This technical improvement allowed watches to become much thinner.

Orologio a ripetizione Vacheron & Constantin prima metà dell'800

Uno dei primi orologi Vacheron & Constantin databile nella prima metà dell'800. Il suono della ripetizione è ottenuto non più da campane, ma con dei gongs. Perfezionamento tecnico, questo, che ha permesso una notevole riduzione dello spessore.

Gold and Enamel Watch,

The ena4meling technique known as *champlevé* consisted of engraving the metal to form a number of closed fields, which were then filled in with enamel paste and fired. After firing, the jeweler removed the excess enamel, before going on to polish the piece. The varying thickness of the enamel on the engraving allowed subtle and refined decorative effects.

Orologio in oro e smalto 1840-50
La tecnica dello smalto cosiddetta Champlevè consisteva nell'incidere il metallo e formare tanti spazi chiusi entro cui veniva fuso lo smalto. A fusione avvenuta, l'orafo provvedeva a togliere l'eccesso di smalto prima di passare alla fase di lucidatura. Il diverso spessore dello smalto sull'incisione permetteva di ottenere delle nuances di ricercato effetto estetico.

Watch with Jumper Mechanism,

A curious and rare example of a watch with "jumping" hours. The hour appears in the little window in the 12 o'clock position. The entire dial is occupied by a single off-center minute hand. The guilloche, or architectural ornament, silver dial is fairly typical of nineteenth-century watches.

Orologio a saltarello metà '800

Curioso e raro esemplare di orologio a ore saltanti. L'ora appare nella finestrella posta sulla posizione delle 12. Tutto il quadrante è occupato da una grande lancetta dei minuti decentrata. Il quadrante in argento guilloche è abbastanza tipico della produzione dell'800.

Gold Watch with Engraved Silver Dial,

Throughout almost the entire nineteenth century, the cylinder escapement was the most widely used type. It allowed the entire mechanism to be flattened enough so that the wearer could slip the watch into a waistcoat pocket. Since decoration all but disappeared after the French Revolution, watchmakers often lavished their talents on sophisticated engraving for the dial.

Orologio in oro quadrante in argento lavorato metà '800 circa

Durante quasi tutto l'800 lo scappamento a cilindro fu il sistema maggiormente utilizzato. Esso infatti permetteva l'appiattimento dell'intero meccanismo consentendo al proprietario di riporre l'orologio all'interno del taschino. Con la Rivoluzione francese tutte le decorazioni scompaiono e l'estro del fabbricante si sfoga spesso in una raffinata incisione del quadrante.

Gold and Enamel Swiss Watch,

MID-19TH CENTURY

*A*nother technique for applying enamel was called *basse-taille*. A uniform layer of transparent monochromatic enamel was applied over a design carved in low relief into the metal, precisely outlining its contours and scrolls.

Orologio svizzero in oro e smalto metà '800
Un'ulteriore tecnica nell'applicazione dello smalto è quella cosiddetta basse-taille. Qui una superficie uniforme di smalto trasparente monocroma ricopre una decorazione cesellata sul metallo, delimitandone esattamente i contorni e le volute.

Heart-Shaped Gold and Enamel Watch,

Since the earliest days, watches had taken a wide variety of shapes. In the most highly prized models, the movement itself conformed to the shape of the case and of the object it was intended to represent. Here the heart shape is adorned with a miniature and a *champlevé* enamel frame.

Orologio in oro e smalti a forma di cuore metà '800
Fin dall'epoca più antica gli orologi da persona presero le forme più diverse. Nei modelli più preziosi il movimento viene sagomato a seconda della conformazione della cassa e dell'oggetto che essa voleva rappresentare. Qui la forma a cuore è impreziosita da una miniatura e da una cornice in smalto Champlevè.

Vacheron & Constantin Watch,

*I*n imposing watches by prestigious makers, even the dome, or back inner dust cap, was made of gold, sometimes more attractively embellished than the case itself. In this period it was not uncommon even for famous-name watches to have a rigorously anonymous dial, bowing to a fashion for scientific rationalism.

Orologio Vacheron & Constantin 1850 circa
Negli orologi importanti, di marche di prestigio, anche la cuvette interna parapolvere veniva realizzata in oro ed era supporto di decorazioni a volte più piacevoli della stessa cassa esterna. In quest'epoca non è inusuale trovare orologi, anche di marche di grande importanza, che si presentano con quadrante rigorosamente anonimo in ossequio ai dettami di una moda di razionalità e scientificità.

Watch with Miniature and Fine Enamel,

LATE 19ᵀᴴ CENTURY

*A*nother method of decoration in the late nineteenth century was to arrange a miniature in the center of the rear cover, while the remaining surface of embossed gold was ornamented with precious stones. Here the result is rather labored and tends to overwhelm the delicate enameled scene.

Orologio con miniatura e smalto fine '800

Altro esempio di decorazione sul finire del XIX secolo fu il restringersi della miniatura nella parte centrale del coperchio posteriore. La superficie rimanente in oro sbalzato era decorata con pietre preziose. Qui il risultato è abbastanza lezioso e tende a soffocare la preziosità della scenetta rappresentata nello smalto.

Sector Watch,

*U*nusually shaped watches have always been a part of watchmaking history. This one, from the early twentieth century, is fan-shaped. For a more accurate resemblance, it offers a sector dial in which the hands execute not a full 360° turn but only half a turn, after which they spring back to the start. The movement is also fan-shaped.

Sector Watch 1910 circa

Gli orologi di forma sono sempre stati presenti nella storia dell'orologio da persona fin dalle sue origini. Questo dell'inizio '900 è fatto a forma di ventaglio e, per meglio imitare l'oggetto che lo ha ispirato, utilizza un quadrante a settore ove le lancette non compiono un giro completo a 360°, ma solo mezzo giro e alla fine del quale tornano di scatto all'inizio. Anche la meccanica è a forma di ventaglio.

English Full-Calendar Watch,

EARLY 20ᵀᴴ CENTURY

*A*n example of a so-called complicated watch. Besides the hour, the watch displays four further functions: the month, day of the month, from 1 to 31, day of the week, and phase of the moon.

Orologio inglese a calendario completo inizio '900
L'orologio a calendario completo è un orologio a complicazioni. Più esattamente vuol dire che oltre all'ora, l'orologio segna altre quattro funzioni: il giorno del mese da 1 a 31, il mese, il giorno della settimana, le fasi lunari.

International Watch,
1 9 1 0

A typical twentieth-century timepiece with a
smooth gold case, enamel dial, easily legible Arabic
numerals, and Breguet hands.

International Watch 1910
*Orologio tipico del XX secolo, cassa liscia in oro,
quadrante in smalto, cifre arabe molto leggibili, sfere
Breguet.*

Triple Complicated Watch with Chronograph,

CIRCA 1900

*I*n addition to a full perpetual calendar and a repeating mechanism to strike the hours, quarters, and minutes, this example also has a chronograph, a complex and precise relative of the stopwatch. The long center hand can be stopped and started to indicate intervals down to a fifth of a second. However complicated, the movement is harmoniously organized, and the lever mechanism is hand-finished.

Orologio a grande complicazione e cronografo 1900 circa

Questo esemplare oltre al calendario completo, perpetuo ed alla ripetizione ore, quarti e minuti, aggiunge anche il cronografo cioè una sfera supplementare centrale che si aziona a scatto per la rilevazione di tempi fino al quinto del secondo. La meccanica si rivela, pur nelle sue complicazioni, armoniosa e i particolari dei leveraggi sono rifiniti a mano.

Patek Philippe Watch,

*P*atek Philippe was probably the most prestigious of all the watchmaking companies. This example, with an extremely simple dial, opens up to reveal a superbly designed and carefully built movement. Note the many separate bridges and the micrometric adjustment of the regulator index.

Patek Philippe 1910 circa
La Patek Philippe fu probabilmente la più prestigiosa fra le ditte costruttrici di orologi. Questo prodotto, dal quadrante estremamente semplice, rivela una meccanica particolarmente curata e di altissima qualità di progettazione. Notiamo, infatti, numerosi ponti separati e la regolazione micrometrica della racchetta del tempo.

Patek Philippe Watch,

CIRCA 1910

*P*restige watches were accompanied by a certificate of guarantee that specifically identified the timepiece and the inspections it had passed before shipping. In the early 1900s, Gondolo Labourian was the Patek Philippe importer for all of Latin America.

Patek Philippe 1910 circa
Gli orologi di pregio venivano accompagnati da un certificato di garanzia ove veniva identificato specificamente l'esemplare ed i controlli che aveva subito prima di essere consegnato. Agli inizi del '900 Gondolo Labourian era l'importatore della Patek Philippe per tutta l'America Latina.

Automatic Watch,

The automatic watch freed the owner from the labor of having to wind it constantly and offered the watchmaker the advantage of a perfectly closed movement. The most widely used mechanism was a moving counterweight. Precisely because it was self-winding, it was important that it had a little dial, as this one has, to indicate how much running time the spring had left.

Orologio automatico inizio '900

L'orologio automatico evitava al proprietario la "schiavitù" di doverlo caricare periodicamente e offriva all'orologiaio il vantaggio di avere un meccanismo perfettamente chiuso. Il sistema più usato fu quello di un contrappeso mobile. Proprio perché automatico vi era la necessità, come in questo esemplare, di un quadrantino che indicasse la riserva di carica, cioè la residua carica della molla.

Swiss Triple Complicated Watch,

In addition to a full calendar, this example also has a repeater mechanism for hours, quarters, and minutes. The calendar is perpetual, meaning that the hand indicating the days of the month is designed to allow for the difference in length of the months and even leap years. In practice, this means that one of the mechanisms moves only once every four years.

Orologio svizzero a grande complicazione 1910-20
Oltre al calendario completo questo esemplare è fornito anche di ripetizione, ore, quarti e minuti. Inoltre il calendario è del tipo cosiddetto perpetuo, cioè la lancetta che segna i giorni del mese è programmata per segnare la differente lunghezza dei vari mesi e addirittura l'anno bisestile. In pratica ciò significa che esiste un meccanismo che interviene ogni quattro anni.

Piguet and Capt Watch,
1 9 1 4

$\mathcal{A}$ minute repeater (striking hours, quarters, and minutes), made by the craftsmen Piguet and Capt, famous for the quality of their creations. They worked at Le Brassus in the Joux valley, the cradle of the best Swiss clock making tradition. The design and finish of the high-quality, white-metal movement are exceptional.

Orologio Piguet & Capt 1914

Orologio a ripetizione ore, quarti e minuti, realizzato dai due artigiani Piguet e Capt, famosi per la qualità delle loro creazioni. Operavano a Le Brassus nella valle del Joux, culla della miglior tradizione orologiaia svizzera. Eccellente la progettazione e la rifinitura della meccanica in metallo bianco di altissima qualità.

Roskopf Watch,

1 9 1 0 - 1 5

Commemorative watches were made specifically for certain historic moments; this example spotlights one episode in Italy's short-lived colonial adventure.

Roskopf 1910-15
Ci sono anche gli orologi commemorativi. Specificamente realizzati per un certo momento storico come questo che segnala una tappa dell'avventura coloniale italiana.

Karussel Watch,

*I*n the first quarter of the twentieth century it became fashionable to expose the "beating heart" of the watch—the balance—to view. Displayed here is a special type of balance called a Karussel, because the balance and the escapement rotate. In this aspect they imitate a more prestigious device invented by Breguet, the *tourbillon*.

Orologio a carosello 1915-20

Verso il primo quarto del '900, venne la moda di rendere visibile il cuore pulsante dell'orologio cioè il bilanciere. In questo caso siamo in presenza di un particolare tipo di bilanciere detto carosello, perché il bilanciere stesso e lo scappamento ruotano entro una gabbia ad imitazione del più prestigioso dispositivo inventato da Breguet detto "Tourbillon."

Ulysse Nardin Swiss Watch,

1 9 2 0

Ulysse Nardin, a major producer of marine chronometers, was a house renowned for watches of the most rigorous precision. This example achieves a harmonious balance between the scientific sobriety of the dial and the unmistakable Art Deco style of the ornamentation.

Orologio svizzero Ulysse Nardin 1920
La Ulysse Nardin era una casa assai famosa con una produzione improntata alla più rigorosa precisione. Importante la sua produzione di cronometri da marina. L'esemplare qui riprodotto sposa felicemente la rigorosa scientificità del quadrante con una decorazione chiaramente inspirata alla Art Déco imperante all'epoca.

Longines Watch,

Longines Watch,

1 9 2 0

A chronograph along classic lines, but with an effective and modern combination of burnished steel and brass that anticipates today's styles.

Longines 1920
Cronografo di linee classiche ma con un felice e moderno accostamento di acciaio brunito e ottone che riecheggia il gusto dei tempi di oggi.

94

Chronograph with Minute Repeating Mechanism,

*A*lthough this complicated watch does not have a movement of outstanding quality, it was intended for a high prelate of the church, as witnessed by the potential owner's monogram and a crown with a cross on top.

Cronografo a ripetizione di minuti 1920 circa

Questo esemplare di orologio a complicazione pur non presentando una meccanica di eccellente qualità, era destinato ad un alto prelato. Il monogramma del destinatario e la corona sormontata da una croce, rivelano tale destinazione.

Election Watch,

CIRCA 1920

$\mathcal{W}$atches made in the first decades of the twentieth century often had greatly elongated and enlarged shapes and numerals, as in this elegant piece.

Election 1920 circa
La produzione di orologi dei primi decenni del secolo era tipizzata da forme e da numerazioni spesso esageratamente allungate e ingigantite come questo bellissimo esemplare di raffinata eleganza.

Swiss Medical Chronograph by Longines,

*M*edical chronographs had special dials for taking a patient's pulse. The doctor had only to count a specified number of beats (normally 30), then read off the pulse rate directly.

Cronografo svizzero Longines medicale 1920-30
I cronografi medicali avevano il quadrante adatto alla misurazione delle pulsazioni. I destinatari di questi cronografi erano infatti medici che rilevando un numero predeterminato di pulsazioni (normalmente 30) potevano immediatamente sapere la regolarità del polso del loro paziente.

Repeater with Automatons,
1 9 2 0 - 3 0

This timepiece struck the hours, quarters, and minutes on command, while the figures on the dial moved.

Italian watchmakers' jargon also calls automatons *Jaquesmats*, a word of obscure origin that may have referred to soldiers standing watch on bell towers. In the nineteenth century, *Jaquesmats* were often combined with a further automaton in the lower part of the face, below the hours dial, like the little sculptor here. The repeating mechanism also operates his arm, which taps the hammer as the hour is struck.

Orologio a ripetizione con automi 1920-30

A richiesta questo esemplare batteva le ore, i quarti ed i minuti e contemporaneamente la scena raffigurata sul quadrante si animava. Gli automi sono chiamati anche in gergo "jaquesmats", parola di origine non chiara, che serviva probabilmente a indicare i soldati posti di vedetta sulle torri campanarie.

Nell'800 ai "Jaquesmats" si aggiungeva spesso un ulteriore automa nella parte bassa dell'orologio, sotto il cerchio orario, come in questo caso ove è presente un piccolo scultore. Il meccanismo della ripetizione anima anche il braccio dello scultore che picchia il martello durante tutta la durata del suono dell'ora.

Audemars Piguet Watch,

A chronograph with a split stop-and-start mechanism. This type can measure intermediate times, or two separate and successive events. The double chronograph hand splits when a button is pressed: one hand stops while the other continues. The stopped hand can then be reset to catch up with the moving one so that they continue together.

Audemars Piguet 1920-40

Cronometro sdoppiante o rattrappante. Questo particolare tipo di cronometro permette la rilevazione dei tempi intermedi o comunque la rilevazione di due eventi separati e successivi. La lancetta del cronografo, infatti, una volta avviata, può sdoppiarsi a comando; una lancetta procede la sua marcia mentre l'altra si arresta sdoppiante. Con un successivo comando la lancetta che si è arrestata raggiunge la prima per continuare insieme la rilevazione cronometrica: rattrappante.

Repeater,

CIRCA 1930

Pocket watches rarely diverged from a round shape. This piece is square, intended to stand on a desk as well as fit in a pocket. The button next to the "3" serves to trigger the repeating mechanism.

Orologio a ripetizione 1930 circa
Gli orologi da tasca assai raramente erano di forma diversa dal rotondo. Questo esemplare è di forma quadrata, perché, oltre che ad essere tenuto in tasca, era predisposto per essere appoggiato su una scrivania. Il pulsante in corrispondenza delle 3 serve per l'azionamento del meccanismo di ripetizione.

Watch with Opposing Dials,

There is also a long tradition of watches with two opposing dials; in other words, with a second dial on the back. Often this second dial indicated solar time (as opposed to daylight savings time). In other examples, such as this one, it served for specialized mathematical calculations in various disciplines.

Orologio a due quadranti 1930 circa

Una buona tradizione hanno anche gli orologi a due quadranti contrapposti, cioè con un secondo quadrante posto sul retro. Spesso questo secondo quadrante era utilizzato per indicare l'ora solare. In alcuni casi come in questo esemplare per i calcoli matematici in campi specifici di applicazione.

Splitting-Hand Chronograph,

A very high-precision chronograph. To emphasize its function while simultaneously making it easier to read, this piece has a double dial. The hours are on a smaller dial, while the larger one is devoted to the chronograph.

Cronografo sdoppiante 1930 circa
Cronografo sdoppiante di altissima precisione. Per dare maggiore rilievo alla funzione di questo crono-grafo, ed al contempo migliorarne la lettura, il quad-rante è del tipo multiplo. Più esattamente: le ore sono riportate su un quadrantino, mentre l'ampiezza del quadrante principale è utilizzata dalle sfere del crono-grafo di precisione.

Vacheron & Constantin Watch,

Vacheron & Constantin was one of the most prestigious watchmakers. The design of this dial from the 1930s incorporates an elegant solution in the way the chronograph's seconds scale encircles the hours dial.

Vacheron & Constantin 1930 circa

Vacheron & Constantin è una delle marche di maggior prestigio. Molto felice è la soluzione grafica di questo quadrante anni '30, ove l'indice a binario della grande botteuse del cronografo, attornia l'indice delle sfere delle ore.

Pendant Watch,

$\mathcal{I}$n this era ladies often wore a watch pinned to their collar or bosom. This pendant watch, with a fired enamel and lacquer case, is pure Art Deco.

Pendentif 1930-40
In quest'epoca le donne amavano appuntare l'orologio al bavero o comunque sul petto. Anche questo Pendentif con la cassa rivestita in smalto a fuoco e lacca è in puro stile Déco.

Movado Ermeto and Rolex Princess,

1 9 4 0 - 5 0

During the 1940s women preferred carrying a watch in a purse over wearing it on the wrist. The most common of these tiny traveling clocks was certainly the Movado Ermeto. Another was the famous Rolex Princess.

Movado Ermeto e Rolex Princess 1940-50
Anzichè al polso le donne preferivano in quest'epoca tenere l'orologio dentro la borsetta. Il più diffuso di questi piccoli orologi da viaggio fu certamente il Movado Ermeto. Un'altra versione da viaggio fu il famoso orologio Rolex Princess.

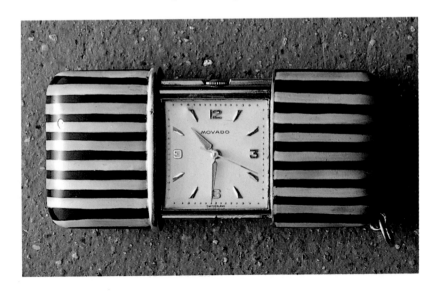

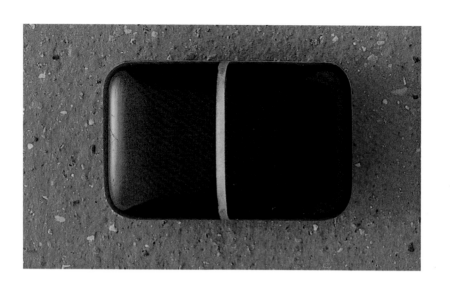

Rolex Prince - Imperial,

1930-40

$\mathcal{T}$he Prince model from Rolex was one of the most famous wristwatches by that firm. But to satisfy more traditional clients who still preferred the pocket watch, Rolex made this elegantly proportioned model,
called Imperial, even though they had no real tradition in this field.

Rolex Prince - Imperial 1930-40
*Il modello Prince della Rolex fu uno dei più famosi orologi da polso prodotti
da questa casa. Per accontentare la clientela più tradizionale ancora legata
all'orologio da tasca, la Rolex, che in questo settore non aveva alcuna
tradizione, realizzò questo modello di proporzioni raffinate ed eleganti che
chiamò Imperial.*

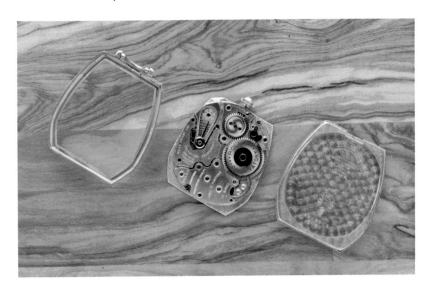

*T*he fashion for ultra-slim wristwatches also spread to the pocket watch in the early 1900s. Shown here are three models that combine technological innovation and contemporary market tastes, with pleasing results.

Ulysse Nardin - Jaeger Le Coultre - Vacheron & Constantin 1920-25
La moda dell'orologio ultrapiatto ha coinvolto nella prima metà del '900 anche l'orologio da tasca. Sono tre esemplari che hanno saputo felicemente sposare l'innovazione tecnologica allo stile ed ai gusti del mercato.

Audemars Piguet - Tiffany

$\mathcal{W}$atches made for evening wear were ornamented with the finest materials. Examples include this elegant Audemars Piguet with a jade case and the Tiffany with platinum and diamonds.

Audemars Piguet - Tiffany
Nelle versioni da sera gli orologi si rivestivano dei materiali più pregiati come questo elegante Audemars Piguet con cassa in giada o il Tiffany in platino e brillanti.

Vacheron & Constantin - Piaget,
1940

*A*round 1940, the pocket watch evolved from its classic shape into an objet d'art, or even an expensive trinket, exemplified by this Piaget set into a coin. Note the clean and classic lines adopted by Vacheron & Constantin in this decade.

Vacheron & Constantin - Piaget 1940
Dalla forma più classica l'orologio da tasca, attorno agli anni '40, diventa anche oggetto d'arte o addirittura prezioso ciondolo, come questo Piaget inserito in una moneta. Nello stesso tempo è da sottolineare la linea essenziale del Vacheron & Constantin degli anni '40.

A Bit of History

The measuring of time was one of the first problems to confront humankind. It arose as soon as we began contemplating the most obvious of astronomical phenomen—the alternation of day and night, the phases of the moon, the seasons. The hours of the day were measured by the varying length of the shadows the sun cast. The moon measured out a longer interval with its varying phases. And, changing foliage and weather signaled the passing of the seasons.

Time was first measured by observing how, as a function of the sun's movement, a person's shadow on the ground changed length from a fixed point of origin. Ancient texts tell us that in the fourth century A.D., the Romans adopted a table of Roman hours measured in "feet of shadow."

At first, the day was divided into two parts: the light part and the dark. Subsequently, each of these segments was divided into twelve equal fractions, called temporary hours. Obviously, their length varied depending on the season and the latitude.

The first instrument made for measuring time was the sundial, either fixed or movable, which told time by the shadow of its pointer, or gnomon. With the help of more or less complex calculations, the use of a sundial made it possible to measure out the course of the day, provided the sun was always shining.

The need to tell time when it was dark led to the invention of other instruments, such as the water clock, the hourglass, and flame systems using candles or oil. These provided at least a rough measurement of the night hours.

THE MECHANICAL CLOCK

The first mechanical clock was probably built in England in 1283, although this date is contested by those from other countries. A weight, suspended from a cord wound around a toothed cylinder, transmitted stored energy to a series of gears that in turn imparted a regular movement to a single indicator hand.

Such clocks were massive turret clocks, which primarily served duty in bell towers. But later they became less bulky and were built to hang on a wall or stand on a table. Still, these clocks had very coarse mechanisms, and only very slowly did their production become more widespread.

In Italy, the construction of Giovanni Dondi's Planetarium in 1364 was of great importance. This instrument, some of whose many indicators were astronomical, represented a real masterpiece of precision engineering.

The weight-driven clock underwent improvements over the years but remained fixed in a single location. Its various models could not be moved at all, much less worn as jewelry. Correspondingly, one of the first goals of mechanical clock making was precisely to create a clock that would work even while it was being moved around. This goal could only be reached by finding a new source of mechanical energy, one capable of being housed within the watch itself.

The search for the proper source of energy was oriented around the spiral spring, which, when wound up, could impart a rotary motion as it unwound. Unfortunately, the results of the many efforts during this very busy period were spottily recorded. We know that Brunelleschi was studying mechanical clocks in 1400, and that Leonardo da Vinci was also interested in the challenge in 1490.

In any case, documents show that by the late fifteenth century, clock-making workshops in Italy were producing mechanical clocks driven by a spring and equipped with a regulating mechanism called a fusee, a kind of toothed cone with a number of grooves that made the spring exert a uniform force.

Once the spiral spring had solved the problem of an autonomous motive force, the clock movement could be enclosed in a container that was not too large to be carried. The first drum watches (so called because of their shape) were made late in the fifteenth century of bronze or gilt brass. Roughly 3 inches in diameter and 4 inches high, weighing perhaps 7 or 10 ounces, they were carried in a little bag tied to the belt or around the neck. Typically, these watches had a single hand on their top face, a dial marked off radially with Roman numerals, and no protective cover. Later, a sturdy ring was added by which they could be hooked to a stout chain. All the elements were in place for what could now truly be called watches. Henceforth, watches would undergo a continuous process of innovation and aesthetic refinement.

The clock makers of Nuremberg devoted considerable effort to the specific problems of clocks to be worn on one's person. In particular, they improved one of the trickiest components of the watch—the spiral spring—which had to be extremely thin and perfectly uniform over its entire length. Later, it became possible to make the spring narrower, and consequently to reduce the outer dimensions of the watch. The original drum shape flattened out, approaching the onion or oval shape; the latter was particularly favored in Nuremberg. Covers were also added to protect the hand.

Another innovation was to reduce the size of the fusee, which was now paired with a miniature chain instead of the hog bristle that had formerly caused a good deal of trouble. Gradually the watch was becoming more accurate and reliable.

PRODUCTION FLOURISHES

*A*ll through the sixteenth and seventeenth centuries, watchmakers created superb specimens. Engraved casings and precious decorations were common. Shapes became smaller and smaller, and, in addition to the traditional oval and onion types, there were watches shaped like spheres, stars, octagons, flowers, and even—for ecclesiastic patrons—crosses. Cases were cast in brass, bronze, or, less often, silver. After roughly 1650, special marks had to be applied to English-made cases: the craftsman's initials, the purity of the metal, and the mark of the assay office. In other watchmaking countries, too, craftsmen began applying their own names to the most visible parts, thus making each piece more valuable. Additional gears were added to the watch to provide more information about time, although the minute hand still lay in the future. As early as 1600 or so, watches could indicate the day, month, and phase of the moon.

This was the birth of so-called complicated movements, which would proliferate and evolve over the years. In later centuries, new dials were added, with various extra hands for perpetual calendars, solar and lunar hours, and other unconventional measures of time. The return system—in which hands move along a semicircle, at the end of which they swing back automatically to their starting point—made it possible to indicate the days of the week and of the month. And finally, striking mechanisms were inserted which not only chimed the hour, half-hour, and quarters, but also acted as alarms.

A MAJOR ADVANCE

In 1675 the French watchmaker Thuret applied the spiral spring to the balance and revolutionized the design of the movement. The new device, which replaced the foliot or crossbar balance, made movements more reliably regular, and thus improved accuracy. This triumphant solution was soon adopted by all watchmakers and became well-established in production. Then, in the same period, the inclusion of a second wheel train made it possible to add a hand for the minutes.

In 1730, the fashion of carrying a watch in the waistcoat pocket caught on among the upper classes. The timepiece was hooked to a short, elaborate chain called a chatelaine, from which also hung other ornamental objects that conferred status on the wearer. This was an age of splendor for the pocket watch, which was regularly adorned with precious-metal cases, exquisite engraving, and personalized enamel decorations in a wide variety of colored patterns.

The automaton, an automatic mechanism that watchmakers ingeniously incorporated into the main movement or drove with additional movements, also flourished during this period. A client could order animated scenes of various subjects to suit his own tastes. There were hunting, floral, mythological, and other motifs, and even the occasional erotic item; in the latter case, the censored areas were covered with a lid that moved aside only when the owner activated a mechanism.

Also significant was the evolution of a mechanism known as the balance cock, the front support of the balance, which became the chief ornamental element of the entire movement. It was made entirely by hand of gilt brass, and each one was a tiny masterpiece of the metal piercer's art, a purely unique item.

The predominant watch shape was still the onion, attached by an articulated ring to the chain. The ring was also often finely worked with decorations similar to those on the case. Watch glasses became less deeply concave and were extremely expensive, as they were produced by grinding down a ball of blown glass.

Paralleling with the spread of pocket watches, a kind of traveling clock called a carriage clock also enjoyed great popularity. Substantially larger and sturdier than watches, perhaps 4 inches in diameter, these, too, were aesthetically superb and offered very precise movements.

By early in the eighteenth century, distinctions were developing among different European schools. The English went the way of technical improvement, while the French and Germans channeled their efforts into ornamentation, producing models of great refinement and beauty. Switzerland followed the French school, while Italy, having made so many major contributions since the dawn of European clock making, now had to be contented with a marginal role, offering no significant production of its own.

The watchmaker's profession was always well-protected by the guilds of each country. In France, to qualify for the guild one had to present one's "masterpiece" for examination by the appropriate panel. Such pieces had to be perfectly executed and finished. The candidate also had to prove he owned sufficient equipment to carry on his profession.

In Germany, the guild examinations were even more severe. The watchmaker had to produce two pieces, one of which had to be a watch with an alarm and hour chime.

The powerful English guild enjoyed the king's protection against any foreign clock makers who attempted to set up shop in England. In Switzerland, where women were banned from clock making, the guild was very similar to that in France. The European guilds were suppressed after the French Revolution.

$\mathcal{I}$n the latter half of the eighteenth century, the European schools of clock making still maintained their individual characteristics virtually unchanged. However, the pocket watch was becoming thinner, simpler, and more austere, until it attained the consular style that was to spread and last until the advent of the winding stem in 1842.

During the French Revolution, dials painted with revolutionary symbols and mottoes were common. But after the Revolution, the sumptuously decorated pocket watch regained its popularity in France. It was precisely such watches that the Swiss began producing, exerting a constantly spreading and consistent pressure on their rivals.

Faux watches without a movement were also made in this period, mere engraved and enameled cases designed purely to satisfy the owner's vanity and taste for ostentation.

Toward the end of the nineteenth century, the major European watchmaking countries were England, France, and new arrival Switzerland, whose Genevan school built rather small, slim, finely worked watches. European watches spread throughout the world, and the increased demand stimulated the first industrial production of watches. Industrial manufacture led to the opening of many different markets, which in turn necessitated the production of many types of watches. Watches bound for the Middle East, for example, were fitted with two or even three outer cases to protect the movement against the desert dust. Those made for export to China, on the other hand, had white enameled dials devoid of decoration and with the second hand in the center, because Chinese clients wanted to see the watch's "beating heart."

For rich Indian rajahs, watches were made as rich and complex as possible. They had to be showy and brilliantly colored with enamels, pearls, and precious stones. Likewise, superb examples were produced for the Russian Imperial Court. They were intended for the nobility and military classes, and served as formal exchanges of gifts or as commemoration of particular honors. The famous watchmaker Breguet produced some exquisite pieces for Russian royalty.

THE BURGEONING MARKET

The pocket watch had been a luxury item, reserved for the well-born and the wealthy. But the onset of industrial production and the consequent decline in cost also made watches accessible to the middle class. Even so, the market did not really explode until the mid-nineteenth century.

Watchmakers generally responded to the greatly increased demand in one of two ways. Some produced relatively inexpensive watches that renounced all unnecessary decoration apart from the balance cock, but kept time with reasonable accuracy. Others continued producing costly, high-precision watches with very attentive workmanship, destined for a rich and refined clientele. One group of makers took a middle path, however, combining the two trends. This group consisted of the followers of the famous Breguet, whose products combined accurate movements with harmonious and pure lines.

Breguet's watches, distinguished with a secret signature, had a slightly convex, very slim round case that set an emphasis on the legibility of the narrowly framed dial. The hands and the dial itself were designed on elegantly classic lines and were very clear to read. Breguet contributed some important innovations in the movement, including the first self-winding mechanism, a new lever escapement, and a new spiral mainspring that still bears his name.

By the end of the nineteenth century, the ornamental pocket watch had lost its fascination for wearers, although it lived on as a piece of jewelry, designed with imaginative shapes and a wide variety of decorations and worn as a pendant or brooch. Nonetheless, this was a century of great importance in the history of the watch. In 1800, Arnold built the first pocket chronometer, a timepiece of exceptional precision, for the British Royal Navy. This was the first in a distinguished line of models, which were not intended for the Navy alone. Such models also introduced important new designs over the course of the century, including segmented balance wheels that automatically compensated for changing temperatures. All were of undisputed accuracy.

In 1820, the second hand was introduced in conjunction with the cylinder escapement; it was centered at first and later had its own small dial. In 1842, Philippe built the first stem-winding watch, thus solving the problem of the separate winding key that had vexed watchmakers and owners from the very start. In 1867, Roskopf began mass production of his watch with an anchor escapement. This model was sturdy and reasonably accurate, but above all very convenient and economical, it cost only 20 francs.

The advent of the wristwatch around 1900 marked the beginning of the pocket watch's decline, and it was ultimately supplanted by the newer type. Today, a limited production of pocket watches caters only to a small group of admirers; it seems, perhaps, not ideally suited to our fast-moving times.

Sadly, almost all examples from the very earliest periods have been lost. Only a few very rare pieces remain, conserved in major museums or famous private collections. Nonetheless, thanks to the patient and dedicated work of a large body of collectors, many interesting timepieces from the past three centuries still survive.

Index of Watchmakers